My Life
in Paragraphs

FIND AND TELL YOUR STORIES

by APRIL BELL

ISBN: 979-8-9886276-0-9

TREE of LIFE LEGACIES
Storytelling with Heart

Praise for My Life in Paragraphs

"What a gift this beautiful book will be to the people lucky enough to read and act on it." —*Bernadette Jiwa, bestselling author of* Story Driven

"I've found that by digging deep and sharing our own authentic stories, we can truly transform the loyalty and productivity of our people. Leaders looking to cultivate trust, connection, and a vibrant culture benefit from using the power of sharing stories that align with their values. April Bell's book offers a solid roadmap to help you do just that. It's a useful tool for creating a lasting impact." —*Mike Robbins, bestselling author of* Bring Your Whole Self To Work

"A perfect book for a lot of different situations: Whether you're a memoirist, journaler, fiction writer, or someone wanting to explore and make sense of your own life, this book will help. April's introductory stories are engaging, compelling, and heartwarming. They reveal her expertise and her open-hearted humanity. (We all would enjoy being interviewed by her.) The questions she offers are rich [story] prompts. The book is beautiful as an object. Money well spent. A great gift for a loved one or yourself." —*Michelle Spencer, writer/storyteller*

"As a creative director, I learned early on brands that allow their audiences to feel safe, heard, intelligent and worthy are the ones people love most. April's approach does all of this and her book is a great starting point for people to tell their stories with pride and grace." —*Jon Soto, creative director*

"A fantastic tool for helping people get in touch with deep and interesting aspects of their lives. It's so elegant and fun to use!" —*Diana Rowan, musician and creativity teacher*

"As a scientist, I've spent my life seeing stories in data; this process has taught me to recognize the power in every individual human story." —*Dr. Ann Blake*, *environmental scientist, changemaker, and memoirist*

"I bought this book for myself but enjoyed it so much that I ended up giving my copy to my dad for his birthday. What a great gift for a loved one. In my dad's case, I suggested he use the audio notes function on his phone to record his answers to the prompts, and then we can transcribe later into a little book! I found the book overall very inspirational and loved the opening chapters where the author shares about how reluctant storytellers can engage with the process...and learn to love it!" —*Sandra Harris*, *author*

"I read a lot of storytelling books. I am happy I picked this book up. First of all, it's beautifully written and very practical in giving me the how-to with very easy-to-digest prompts to help unearth my stories. Not only was I informed, I'm inspired. Loved it!" —*Enrika Greathouse*, *creative entrepreneur*

"If you want to feel connected—to yourself, to others, and to the world around you—this book is for you. April Bell assures everyone that their stories matter, and shares heartfelt and practical tips for unearthing them. If you've been curious about personal storytelling but didn't know where to start, or do a lot of public speaking and want to learn the art of inserting vulnerable storytelling into your presentations, or just want to be known and remembered for who you truly are by family members, get this book. You will not be disappointed." —*Rumi Tsuchihashi*, *writer/author*

For Elizabeth, whose wisdom and example made this book possible; and for Carli, my eternal champion of authentic self-expression.

Sample Story Prompts

🌍 **Earth:** Grounding + Values

**Tell of a time you felt you
truly belonged.**

🌿 **Air:** Hopes + Dreams

**Who or what has been a source of
hope for you in your life?**

🔥 **Fire:** Passions + Motivations

**What have you learned
the hard way?**

💧 **Water:** Emotions

**Tell of a time you experienced
your own courage.**

Contents

"Stories carry the seeds of our humanity. They help us, teach us, heal us. And they connect us to each other and to ourselves."

—Mary Oliver

Prelude

I'M LYING IN a hammock in the High Sierra. It's a lazy mid-afternoon. I can feel the warm summer air on my skin. The scent of a nearby Sequoia envelops me. As I bask in serene quiet, I become aware of the wind rushing through the treetops. I tune in as the sound ebbs and flows, the trees telling their collective story—a story of community and connection. My experience is peaceful, comforting, and pure. My hammock drifts from side to side. I feel at home.

I'm moved to ponder my place within our greater human family. I have become the listener and the guide—I am the one to capture your story and help you find its place in our collective human story. I have always seen the value and importance of being a story catcher, and now I, too, must become a storyteller.

As we find the courage to share our stories from the depths of our own hearts, we orchestrate our collective symphony, just like those majestic trees.

What's your story?

—*April Bell ~ Summer 2022*

"To be fully alive, we must be willing to tell our own story, to be vulnerable and honest about who we are and what we've experienced."

—Mark Nepo

Intention

I AIM TO inspire and help you in sharing your personal stories. At the beginning of this book, I tell a few stories of my own, including how I discovered and developed the "My Life in Paragraphs" process. In Part Two, you'll find storytelling tips and tricks, along with the format I use to help individuals and groups discover and share their values-based stories.

My hope is that you enjoy this voyage of self-discovery. My wish is for you to build deeper connections with the people in your life by taking turns sharing and listening to each other's tales. Connecting through story can happen anywhere—around the dinner table with family, in circles with friends, or even in professional settings where sharing your authentic story helps others understand not just what you believe, but why you believe it. In the realm of legacy, it is the stories we tell about our learning experiences, our hopes, our dreams, and how we define our values that reveal who we truly are.

Part One:

Personal Storytelling

"Instructions for living a life:

Pay attention. Be astonished.

Tell about it."

—Mary Oliver

The Reluctant Storyteller

IT'S A BEAUTIFUL fall day, and I'm standing on the porch of Elizabeth's house in the Oakland Hills. With a warm, friendly smile and an excited hello, Peter, her son, swings the front door wide open, inviting me in. I'm there to film his mom telling her life story.

Twelve years earlier, Peter's dad had died of cancer, and Peter's deep regret has been that he never had the chance to record his dad telling his stories in his own voice.

I enter their comfortable home and begin glancing around for a good spot to set up my video camera. Peter calls his mom over and introduces us. Just like her son, Elizabeth is very warm and welcoming. She exudes kindness. While she possesses a regal air, she is extremely down-to-earth. I like her instantly. After greeting me, she turns to face her son more directly, her warm smile dropping away from her face. In a serious tone she says, "Do we really need to do this?"

Uh-oh. My heart sinks as I step away from the two of them and quietly continue going about my setup work. I've been in this scenario before; Elizabeth is what I refer to as "the reluctant storyteller."

I can partially overhear their strained whispers as I'm making myself busy. I hear Peter say, "Mom, I want you to do it for me." At that, Elizabeth lets out an exasperated sigh and leaves the room.

A short while later I have the camera, lights, and sound all set, and Elizabeth rejoins us. Her posture is stiff, with her arms folded across her chest. She has a mildly stern look on her face. She's still resisting the whole affair, and although Peter has chosen a gentle approach, he's holding his ground. I'm aware of being sandwiched between two very strong-willed people, each determined to have their way.

The final task before showtime is to place the microphone on Elizabeth's lapel. This is a very up-close and personal activity, where we are inches apart. I'm trying to put the mic on her, and she's sort of trying to take it off at the same time. It's somewhat comical, and certainly awkward for me. All the while, she continues to offer more objections to her son:

"Why do we even need to do this? I don't have anything interesting to say. I don't even have grandchildren; I have grand-dogs . . . and it seems highly unlikely that's ever going to change."

Peter repeats himself: "Mom, I want you to do it for me and KayMaria. We want to know your story. And I want to have it recorded."

Elizabeth finally concedes, and I'm able to affix the microphone to her lapel. I am relieved when she sits in the chair I've positioned opposite my own.

Peter takes his leave as I settle in directly across from Elizabeth. Instantly, the warm, kind woman I was initially introduced to returns. She thanks me for being there, and I give her a brief overview of how our interview will unfold. I press record and ask my first question.

She shares incredible tales, from her mother coming to America from Greece by way of Egypt and England as a nanny, to her epic love story with Peter's dad. She gushes about their many joyful years shared raising their two children, and tears well up as she recounts the heartbreaking sorrow of her husband's early death. She reads me poetry, shares her hopes and dreams, talks about her complex relationship with her father, and speaks of all the things she holds most dear. Three hours later, Elizabeth is still talking!

When it's finally time to switch off the camera, Elizabeth is aglow and remarks on what a wonderful voyage it has been. She says she had no idea there was so much to share, nor did she realize how her life would look while witnessing it as we did during our time together.

A year or so after our interview, Elizabeth writes to me, thanking me for the experience. She shares that she has been expanding upon the collection of stories we gathered that day by doing a practice she calls "My Life in Paragraphs." Anytime she has a memory or a reminder from her past, she takes a little time to write a paragraph or two about it. Some of these paragraphs she sends to her children or a dear friend. Or she simply saves a cherished memory for herself.

"We're all storytellers from the moment we're born. We're constantly telling ourselves stories about the world, about who we are, about where we come from, about where we're going."

—Thomas King

Why "My Life in Paragraphs"?

WHEN I READ that thank-you note from Elizabeth, I felt overjoyed. I immediately wondered how I could inspire or guide more people to remember and share their personal stories. Telling stories about your life and experiences can seem like a daunting task, but if you take it one story at a time, you'll be amazed at how quickly you can build a rich collection. The stories you unearth might even surprise you, offering a transformative experience.

I often find myself talking to people who have fascinating stories but may not feel ready for a video interview session. I also meet folks interested in getting guidance so they can gather or craft stories on their own. This could be for personal enjoyment, to build a legacy, or to share more authentically in a business setting. When professionals learn to share their personal stories at work, something meaningful happens. Instead of just presenting data or strategies, they share the values and experiences that have shaped their thinking. Colleagues start to understand not only what they believe but also why they believe it. Trust deepens, connections grow, and authentic leadership naturally emerges.

In a world flooded with information, your personal story is what will truly captivate and resonate. Scientific research has shown that people are more likely to remember stories than just data. If you want your idea, guidance, or theory to last, turn it into a story. A well-crafted personal story ignites emotions, helping you tap into empathy. This releases oxytocin in your listener's brain, which makes them see you as more trustworthy.[1]

What better way to leave a lasting impact? Storytelling is a powerful way to communicate what matters most to you. It also boosts the chances that your message will be heard and remembered. Think about the most memorable TedTalks you've seen. I'm willing to bet the speaker's use of a personal story is what hooked you in.

After learning about Elizabeth's "My Life in Paragraphs" practice, I had the epiphany to combine her activity with the idea of the ethical will, which is a way for people to share their wisdom stories (more on that later). You will find in these pages fifty-two thought-provoking story prompts. Also included is my step-by-step storytelling process. I've made it as simple and enjoyable as possible to help you find and share your stories. You can use this process to tell stories live, through video, on audio, or in writing; at home or at work, or as part of a legacy project. The choice is entirely yours.

[1] Owens, Alexandra. "Tell Me Al I Need to Know About Oxytocin." Psycom.net, September 23, 2021. https://psycom.net/oxytocin

"Through personal storytelling, we can create a better understanding of ourselves and others. It's a powerful tool for building community and fostering change."

—Bernadette Jiwa

Your Story Matters

THIS REVELATION MIGHT be a bit surprising, but I've been super averse to telling my own stories in a structured or public way. You see, I'm also a reluctant storyteller. Over the years, people would say to me, "Oh, yeah, you're the storyteller!" to which I would respond, "No, no. I'm the story catcher; **you're** the storyteller!"

In the storytelling workshops I lead, I help people find their stories. As part of my presentation, I do tell stories of my own. From my perspective, I do an okay job, and I've always gotten positive feedback. I also have felt the desire to tell better stories, so I signed up for an online storytelling workshop led by a master storyteller. The juicy part was sharing stories within our cohort of students, giving and receiving feedback. It was quite a powerful process.

To be honest, my second time in the course was when I finally got what I had come for. In my first go, the previous year, I couldn't get out of my own way. I showed up to that first effort with a vision and an agenda I was really attached to. In hindsight, I saw my error. When embarking on effort two, I chose to go in with the intention of being in it for the fun. The big gift from that shift was that I realized if I could hold my stories lightly, without being overly significant about them, they would flow out of me. This was a major breakthrough for me. And what I found on the other side of that breakthrough was the deep gift that the many layers of personal storytelling can be for storytellers themselves.

One of the stories I shared with my group was about a crossroads moment in my life. Back in 2008, when I launched Tree of Life Legacies—my video storytelling business—I found myself in need of a job so I could make money while I got my wisdom-keeping project off the ground.

After a few twists and turns, I found myself with the choice between a safe and stable government job or driving the drink cart at the local golf course. The stability of the government job was appealing to me. The fun of the drink cart gig was also attractive. The thing was, I knew if I took that government job, I would find my way to the leadership track, with all its benefits and retirement perks, leaving my storytelling business on the shelf. At the golf course, this would not be the case; the odds of that job shape-shifting into a career track were pretty slim. So I chose the golf course, and here I am today.

Rumi, a woman I befriended in the workshop, heard my

story and offered her feedback. She said that my story hit really close to home. She had recently left a dream-stalling government job herself in order to take her writing business to the next level. She said:

". . . after I quit that government job, I spoke with my favorite intuitive counselor, who encouraged me to keep an eye out for a supplemental income job that I could do for the fun of it. I couldn't even imagine what such a thing would look like. Then I read about your golf cart job and went, 'Ooh, like THAT.'"

Within a few months of our exchange, I received an announcement that she had published her first book, which I immediately ordered!

Stories have power.

They help us understand

ourselves, our world, and

our place in it."

—Laura Packer

What Is Personal History?

S O THERE IT was. I finally got the thing I'd spent years evangelizing: MY stories matter! I'll never know which part of my story will make a difference. And that's exactly what I want you to understand—your stories matter too. Not just the polished ones or the obviously meaningful ones, but all of them. You never know which detail, which moment, which choice will be exactly what someone else needs to hear. Even if I have an agenda or a point to make with how and where I share a story, there's always the potential for that little spark; what I see as a random detail could be the nudge that connects and creates a meaningful impact in someone else's life.

This is exactly why I encourage professionals to share personal stories at work. That golf cart story? I've shared it with colleagues and clients when talking about decision-making and staying true to your values. People remember it because it shows how I genuinely think and what influences my choices. It's one thing to say I value passion over security—it's another to tell the story of choosing the golf cart over the government job. Personal stories don't just convey your message; they reveal who you truly are.

When I started working as a personal historian in 2008, I realized that people loved the idea but were generally unaware of this growing profession. Have you ever wondered what a personal history is, who does one, or why people even do this?

Sir Winston Churchill said, "History shall be kind to me, for I intend to write it." Who better to document a person's history than the individual who actually experienced the events?

I'd like to invite you to participate in a small exercise. It's simple, and if you give yourself the space to pause and think about the prompts, it could be enlightening.

- Think back to an important person from your past—a relative or a mentor—someone you admire.

- With eyes closed, take a few deep breaths, and reflect on what you appreciate about this person.

- Pause

- How would it feel if you could have these thoughts, feelings or memories about them preserved so others could experience and learn from them, too?

That's essentially the idea behind recording personal history. Simple, yet deeply meaningful.

The reasons people create personal histories are varied. They may want to:

- explain their ancestry

- celebrate an event

- memorialize a person

- create a time capsule for a growing child

- communicate their decision-making process

- record what the world is like

- communicate their past to the future

Memories are sometimes recorded as a tribute to courage, or kindness, or generosity of spirit. Sometimes they're told to set the record straight or create a sense of community. Many stories collected through personal histories focus on an ordinary person's experience of extraordinary events in their life—personal or historical. The process is almost always a journey of self-discovery—a way to make sense of your life and past while reflecting on what you've learned along the way. It can serve as a guidepost on the path leading to where you'd like to go next. There's value in doing it at any age!

The Many Layers of Personal Storytelling

THERE ARE MANY layers to personal storytelling. Here's a collection of aspects I find inspiring.

FUN: One thing I've learned over the years is that telling stories is fun! Even if you're just telling for yourself. You might be surprised by who ends up interested in your tales. Often, it's not who you'd expect. People don't always take away what you think they will. But that's part of the magic. I love seeing someone's face light up when a story hits them in an unexpected way. Suddenly, you're having conversations you never thought you'd have, connecting with people in new and authentic ways.

SELF-EXPLORATION: I know this might seem a little touchy-feely to some—and honestly, the term "self-exploration" can feel somewhat self-indulgent. But here's what I've noticed: when you take time to really look at your life and acknowledge what you've been through and what has mattered to you, something interesting happens. It's like taking inventory, but in a gentle way. And paradoxically, when you give yourself permission to understand your own story, you become more present and available to others. Knowing yourself creates space to truly see the people around you.

SELF-EXPRESSION: We all have a deep need to feel heard, to tell our story in our own words. When we do, it's truly fulfilling. It takes courage because that gremlin choir can be loud—you know, those naughty little voices that try to tell you where and how you've failed, that inner-meanie that says, "No one wants to hear this!" Once those little monsters are put in the corner where they belong, and your focus shifts to your trials and triumphs, your learning experiences and turning points, telling your own story becomes incredibly illuminating, engaging, and fun.

SELF-ILLUMINATION: Something wonderful happens once you've gathered even a small collection of stories—you start to see patterns in your life. Your strengths, your struggles, where you've grown and why. Who's been there for you, and who hasn't.

Our reluctant storyteller, Elizabeth, shared something inspiring with me after we recorded her stories. At seventy, she said the process gave her a wonderful gift. Reflecting on her life's twists and turns helped her think about what she wanted to do next. She knew she had a finite number of years left to enjoy, and engaging in the process of recording her stories helped her focus on how she wanted to spend her precious remaining time.

Gaining these kinds of insights can be truly special, even if they're not always easy to find. I uncovered something about my own story that I hadn't realized before. While piecing together the origin story for Tree of Life Legacies, it suddenly hit me—my dad was the one who first planted the seeds for my business, long before I even started it. He was the first to share the vision of it with me. When that realization hit, I felt deeply moved. I'm so thankful he's still alive so I can thank him for his valuable gift. Honestly, there's nothing else I'd rather be doing with my life.

CONNECTION: Here's something that might surprise you—I believe the most important skill of a good storyteller is being a good listener. We learn so much simply by listening, though it's not always as easy as it sounds. True listening means giving someone your full attention, staying present in the moment, and genuinely hearing not just their words but what lies beneath them. It means not interrupting or judging, but allowing the person to express themselves freely. When you listen this way, you notice things you might otherwise miss—the deeper meaning behind their words.

Connection starts with this kind of listening. When we share our stories and truly listen, new conversations open up, understanding deepens, and trust grows. Our ability for empathy expands. Dr. Brené Brown explains it well when she says connection is "the energy that exists between people when they feel seen, heard, and valued." I've seen this kind of connection change workplaces, too. When team members share stories about what motivates them or the challenges they've faced, instead of just working alongside each other, people start working together. They understand not only what their colleagues do but what drives them to do it well. These shared stories build a foundation of understanding that helps everything else—problem-solving, creativity, difficult conversations—all flow more smoothly. In a world full of noise, being a good listener is a rare and precious gift.

ALCHEMY: This is where something powerful happens that I never could have predicted when I began this work. Simply by sharing and listening, everyone involved seems to change a little. Elizabeth, our reluctant storyteller in the earlier tale, discovered things about herself she hadn't realized. I found myself viewing my own story differently simply by witnessing hers. It's this quiet magic that happens when we're brave enough to be vulnerable and generous enough to truly listen. That's the fifth element in my process—the gentle alchemy that naturally unfolds when stories are shared with an open heart.

"The stories we tell ourselves and each other help us understand who we are and what we value. They help us create meaning in our lives."

—Mark Nepo

What is an Ethical Will?

WHEN RUMI'S BOOK arrived, I was thrilled to discover it was actually an ethical will, which made perfect sense to me, given how deeply I had been moved by it. I first learned about ethical wills in 2008, and they've been at the heart of everything I do ever since. They offer a way for people to find and tell their values-based stories.

If you're confused by that term, you're not alone. I've spent years trying to find a different name for it, as have many others. I eventually looked up its origin. "Ethical" comes from the Greek word ethos, meaning "way of living." A will, as most of us understand, describes how someone wants their possessions divided after they pass away. So, it stands to reason, an ethical will is simply a way to share how you've chosen to live your life and why.

Ethical wills are a centuries-old Jewish tradition and a meaningful way to pass on your values and philosophies, your hard-won wisdom, and the lessons you've learned. Sometimes, people use an ethical will to share their hopes and dreams; other times, it's used to express regrets or apologies. Whatever the purpose, these stories offer inspiration, guidance, and hope.

Nothing is more powerful than the human story. When we share our struggles and celebrations—our failures and successes—we connect in ways far beyond possessions or achievements. Your values-based stories—your ethical will—are your chance to show people who you truly are. You have a perspective no one else has. Don't let that go unshared. Record it on video or audio, write it down, or choose any medium that speaks to you.

"The purpose of a
storyteller is not to
tell you how to think,
but to give you questions
to think upon."

—Brandon Sanderson

"Stories are like
breadcrumbs. They lead
us where we need to go,
and they nourish us
along the way."

—Mark Nepo

"My Life in Paragraphs" Concept

INSPIRED BY MY fascination with the ethical will, I created "My Life in Paragraphs" as a process and collection of fifty-two thought-provoking story prompts to help you share the stories that give your life meaning and purpose. The prompts are organized into four themes, with thirteen questions in each. When you see the icon at the top of the page, it indicates which theme the prompt belongs to:

 Earth: Grounding + Values

 Air: Hopes + Dreams

 Fire: Passions + Motivations

 Water: Emotions

These four elements make up the core of your stories—the heart of what you share. But from the root of earth, through the breath of air, the fire of will, and the flow of water, emerges Alchemy: the sacred art of becoming. This fifth element captures the profound changes that happen when we choose to share our stories and listen attentively to others. It's the magic that happens when we're able to find new parts of ourselves through the mirror of being truly heard.

Alchemy

Many of the prompts include a follow-up question, which can help you explore your story more deeply.

If you decide to use the "My Life in Paragraphs" process I've included in the next section (page 156), be aware that it is designed to be contemplative. Take your time and enjoy the process. Go one step at a time, one story at a time. Before long, you'll be pleased to see your collection of meaningful stories has grown.

This process is most effective when done with another person or in a small group. I've provided guidance on how to do story work with others in Part Two of this book. Hearing others' stories and listening as they process their story ideas will help you clarify your own. The key details you want to craft into your stories will come to light more easily when working with a story circle or a trusted friend.

"Stories are a way of sharing

our experiences, our hopes,

our dreams, and our fears.

They help us to connect with

one another, to see the world

through someone else's eyes,

and to learn from

one another."

—Thomas King

The "My Life in Paragraphs" process is designed for people who might not love writing but still enjoy exploring their experiences and expressing their values through personal stories. The Story Notes section on the left of each prompt can be used to create a "beat sheet" (page 166) or to jot down bullet-point notes about your story.

How you engage with the book is completely up to you. I suggest browsing through these pages and choosing a prompt that sparks your interest in the moment. You can also challenge yourself (and/or your story circle) by randomly flipping to a page and diving into stories that way.

Remember to be gentle with yourself during this process. Some stories or prompts may bring up difficult memories. If strong emotions become too overwhelming to handle alone, seeking professional support is always a wise choice. Keep in mind that the main goal of this book is to be your companion and guide as you discover the joy of exploring your personal wisdom and stories.

Life Story Prompts

Grounding + Values

Story Notes:

Tell of a time when you felt you truly belonged.

Was it with an individual
or a community? A place?

Story Notes:

What biases or prejudices have you transcended?

Tell what prompted you to change.

Story Notes:

_____

_____

_____

_____

_____

_____

_____

_____

_____

_____

_____

_____

_____

_____

_____

_____

_____

_____

What is one of the hardest things you have ever done?

Which of your core values are
illustrated in the story?

Story Notes:

How are you a product of your time in history?

Which of your core values are illustrated in this story?

Story Notes:

Who has been a strong influence in your life?

Which of your core values are
influenced by them?

Story Notes:

What disadvantage from your past do you now view as a benefit?

Which of your core values have
been shaped by this?

Story Notes:

Who have you forgiven or who has forgiven you?

Why is this important?

Story Notes:

What are some beliefs you hold as truths?

What experiences generated
those beliefs?

Story Notes:

Tell of a core value influenced by one or both of your parents.

Is there a specific experience that generated that value for you?

Story Notes:

_____

_____

_____

_____

_____

_____

_____

_____

_____

_____

_____

_____

_____

_____

_____

_____

_____

_____

What loss or losses have shaped who you are today?

Which of your values are reflected in this story?

Story Notes:

_____

_____

_____

_____

_____

_____

_____

_____

_____

_____

_____

_____

_____

_____

_____

_____

_____

Tell of a time you were deeply moved by the kindness of another.

How did this change you?

Story Notes:

Tell of a time when you felt truly valued.

How did this change you?

Story Notes:

_____

_____

_____

_____

_____

_____

_____

_____

_____

_____

_____

_____

_____

_____

_____

_____

_____

Tell of a hardship you have faced.

How has this shaped you?

Life Story Prompts

Hopes + Dreams

Story Notes:

When you were a child, what did you want to be when you grew up?

Are you happy or sad that it did
or did not happen?

Story Notes:

_____

_____

_____

_____

_____

_____

_____

_____

_____

_____

_____

_____

_____

_____

_____

_____

_____

_____

If you're a parent or guardian, what hopes did you have for your young child/ren?

What hopes do you have for them today?

Story Notes:

_____

_____

_____

_____

_____

_____

_____

_____

_____

_____

_____

_____

_____

_____

_____

_____

_____

_____

_____

Who or what has been a source of hope for you in your life?

How has this sustained you?

Story Notes:

For whom would you like to be a source of hope?

How so?

Story Notes:

_____

_____

_____

_____

_____

_____

_____

_____

_____

_____

_____

_____

_____

_____

_____

_____

_____

_____

_____

Are you a person of faith?

What does your faith mean to you?

Story Notes:

How would you like to be remembered?

What actions do you take
to serve this desire?

Story Notes:

_____

_____

_____

_____

_____

_____

_____

_____

_____

_____

_____

_____

_____

_____

_____

_____

_____

_____

_____

_____

Is there anything you wish you had done differently?

What, why, and how?

Story Notes:

Do you believe in an afterlife?

What do you think happens
after we die?

Story Notes:

What family traditions do you most value?

Which ones do you hope the
children in your family continue?

Story Notes:

What guidance would you give young couples today?

What relationship advice do
you wish you'd been offered
as a young person?

Story Notes:

What would you like your legacy to be?

How are you living your life today
to support that desire?

Story Notes:

What guidance would you give a young person on how to have a happy life?

What advice do you wish you'd been offered as a young person?

Story Notes:

What life experiences do you most hope others get to have?

What are some of your most
enjoyable life experiences?

My Life in Paragraphs

Life Story Prompts

Passions + Motivations

Story Notes:

Tell of a time you overcame the odds.

What moved you through
the experience?

Story Notes:

Tell about the first time you fell in love.

What thoughts/feelings do you recall when you knew you were in love?

Story Notes:

What motivates you into action?

What does it take for you to act?

Story Notes:

How did
you meet your
significant other?

When did you know they
were "the one" for you?

Story Notes:

What have you learned the hard way?

What guidance would you give another to spare them going through that experience?

Story Notes:

Have you ever felt like you had the rug pulled out from under you?

How did you manage
that experience?
How has it shaped you?

Story Notes:

How have you made the world a better place?

What meaning does this
hold for you?

Story Notes:

Have you ever done the right thing, even though it was the harder thing?

Why did you make that choice?

Story Notes:

What have been
some of your hobbies
over the years?

Why did each thing
hold your interest?

Story Notes:

What are some of the best times with your significant other?

Which times were the
most difficult?

Story Notes:

What have you learned about life from being in love?

How has this shaped you?

Story Notes:

What have you learned from your longest friendships?

Do you have guidance
for others on keeping
long-term friendships?

Story Notes:

How have you been mischievous in your life?

As a child?
As an adult?

Life Story Prompts

Emotions

Story Notes:

Tell of a time you felt incredibly happy.

What or who caused this?

Story Notes:

Tell of a time you felt afraid and how you got past it.

What did you learn about yourself?

Story Notes:

Tell about a moment when you have felt a deep sense of love and connection.

Who were you with, and what were you doing?

Story Notes:

What has made
you angry
and why?

How do you express your anger?

Story Notes:

What are you grateful for?

Why?

Story Notes:

Tell of a time you were deeply disappointed.

How did you get through it?

Story Notes:

Tell of a time you felt sadness or grief. What sustained you during this time?

What have you learned from your own grief or sadness?

Story Notes:

Tell of a time when
you were left
surprised, amazed,
or awestruck.

Story Notes:

Tell about a person you greatly admire.

How has this person shaped
who you are today?

Story Notes:

_____

_____

_____

_____

_____

_____

_____

_____

_____

_____

_____

_____

_____

_____

_____

_____

_____

_____

When or with whom have you experienced tenderness?

How has this changed
or affected you?

Story Notes:

Tell of your favorite pet(s).

What did you learn about
love from your pet?

Story Notes:

What have you learned about love from being a parent or guardian?

How has this shaped
who you are today?

Story Notes:

Tell of a time when you experienced your own courage.

What happened?
Did this change you?

PART TWO EXPLORES the fifth element of the "My Life in Paragraphs" process:

◎ Alchemy

Here you'll discover how sharing your stories can lead to deep change—not just for your listeners, but most powerfully for yourself. This is where the sacred art of becoming unfolds—where storytelling moves beyond simply recounting and becomes a catalyst for growth, healing, and greater self-awareness.

While Earth, Air, Fire, and Water symbolize the four categories of stories you'll explore through the prompts, Alchemy reflects what can happen not only when you contemplate them, but when you share them. It represents the potential for deep shifts that occur when we move from silently carrying our stories inside to speaking them out loud. Throughout this section, you'll notice how the simple act of sharing stories—whether with a friend, in a group, or through technology—can sometimes bring about unexpected moments of growth and connection for everyone involved.

Part Two:

Finding and Telling Your Stories

"The most powerful person
in the world is the storyteller.
The storyteller sets the vision,
values, and agenda of an entire
generation that is to come"

—Steve Jobs

StoryCatcher®

JULIAN, A FORTY-ISH charming and quite dapper businessman, is standing in front of me. With a lilting French accent, he says,

"I really love your business. I feel it has so much value. I was thinking . . . you know what you really need?"

His manner is so warm and inviting, my attention is fully rapt. I tilt my head ever so slightly and raise my eyebrows, gesturing for him to say more.

"You need to create an app for it!"

Puzzled, I simply stare at him. His eyes are sparkling. He's aglow, inspired by his brilliant idea for me. He's clearly anticipating the same light bulb that's gone on for him to go on for me. It's not happening, though. I have no idea what he's talking about. I ask him to explain further, and he says, "Do you know about Angry Birds?"

I say, "Nooo . . ."

This is 2011, and I'm not very up on apps or smartphones, even though I have one.

"It's a game my kids play on their iPhones. It's insanely

popular," he proclaims. Maintaining his passion and kind conviction, he urges, "It's an app! You need to make an app for what you do!"

Moments later, I still have no idea what he's talking about when our attention is pulled elsewhere.

Once back home, I download the Angry Birds app on my iPhone and play a few rounds. Now I'm totally confused. My business focuses on capturing people's life stories on video. How in the world that even remotely relates to a game that consists of slingshotting animated birdlike bombs for points is absolutely beyond me. I turn off my iPhone, switch off the lights, and go to sleep.

The next day, back in the workshop Julian and I are both taking in San Francisco, that light bulb all of a sudden goes on. Looking back, I have no idea how. I can only credit this to being in a personal growth and development workshop. Those spaces generally lend themselves to expansive thinking.

Julian's idea solved a problem I'd been exploring ever since I began capturing life stories. Often I'd meet people who had lived incredible lives but didn't always have the means to hire me, or they weren't quite ready to engage in the larger task of telling their full story. I was super interested in finding a do-it-yourself process that would make sharing personal stories simple and accessible to anyone interested in doing so. Finally, the solution had revealed itself!

There was only one problem . . . I'm not a coder. Back in those days, a person with zero programming skills with an app idea was tasked with assembling a team and manifesting the $50,000-plus in funding needed to bring their idea to market. This entailed jumping through a lot of hoops, juggling a lot of balls, and, for many, a solid dose of heartbreak.

One of my repeating patterns is that when a problem arises, life often presents a solution. As luck would have it, one of my closest friends, Urs, was a talented programmer who began coding iPhone apps in 2009. I called him the very next day to pitch my idea.

I was giddy with excitement as I shared my vision with him. I proposed we make a simple and easy tool, including great questions to ask, that would help people capture their personal stories on video. It would be set up so the user could add photos, screen text, and a title card. Voila! Anyone could be the documentarian in their family or circle of friends, using a device most already carried in their purse or pocket.

After I finished illustrating my vision, Urs scratched his chin and stared up into the heavens for a good while, clearly analyzing if it was possible. He then said, "Well, that's a very interesting idea. Rendering the videos will be challenging to figure out, but let's try it!"

I was delighted. We held a mutual intention to leverage technology to generate more love and connection in people's lives through video storytelling, a hopeful redirection from where tech seemed to be going. We also felt committed to honoring people's privacy, and we chose the rogue route of omitting any sort of data collection.

For the next two-and-a-half years, we developed, tested, and reworked our app. Finally, as a team of two with zero investors, we accomplished what many well-funded teams struggled with and sometimes failed to do. In September of 2013, we launched StoryCatcher® Pro on The Apple App Store. I was over the moon some months later when a reporter from The New York Times called, wanting to include our app in a piece on ethical wills being revamped for the tech age.

The criticism we received from marketers and entrepreneurs for our choice to omit data collection was sometimes difficult to take (for me, not Urs). As the years have worn on, it turns out our respect for people and their privacy has proved to be the right choice. For ten years and running, our app has helped thousands worldwide capture and share their most cherished stories on video.

"In a world that often seems chaotic and confusing, stories give us a way to make sense of things. They help us to find meaning and purpose, and to navigate our way through life."

—Thomas King

"We all have stories worth telling, stories that can help people feel less alone and more connected. When we share our stories, we open up space for others to share theirs too."

—Brené Brown

Create an MLP Group

NOW THAT SOME provocative prompts have inspired you to find your stories, I encourage you to seek out a trusted story buddy or create a sacred storytelling circle. As you share your stories, you'll support each other when you get stuck. Sharing in a group offers a safe way to receive helpful feedback as you develop your tales. It's therapeutic and helps you connect with others in meaningful ways. Hearing others' stories and sharing your own is the most inspiring way to discover and refine what truly matters to you.

MLP Group Guidelines

IF YOU CHOOSE to create a storytelling circle or group to go through the "My Life in Paragraphs" process, I've put together some guidelines to help everyone feel safe and supported. Share these guidelines at the start of each session to make sure everyone is on the same page and feels taken care of.

CONFIDENTIALITY: Let's agree to create a safe and sacred space for sharing our stories.

- Does everyone agree to keep everything said or shared here confidential?

- Raise your hand or indicate if you cannot keep this promise.

Respectfully invite anyone unable to agree to confidentiality to remove themselves from the group.

BE SUPPORTIVE: Personal storytelling isn't a space for judging others. The secret sauce to a good story is vulnerability, which takes courage. When you allow a storyteller to feel supported and heard, everyone will have a more meaningful experience.

MIND THE TIME: Make sure everyone has enough time to share. The best way to do this is to assign a "Minder of the Time." Use a smartphone app or a sand timer. Give each person in the group the same amount of uninterrupted time. Use a soft bell or chime to give a thirty-second warning so the teller knows it's time to wrap up.

BE RESPECTFUL: Avoid giving unsolicited advice. Provide coaching only when asked. Keep in mind that you may not know the story behind the story, so everyone is strongly encouraged to avoid passing judgment or offering advice.

BE A GOOD LISTENER: Sometimes, all a storyteller needs is to hear their story told out loud. They might find the answers and insights they are looking for through your gift of listening. Keep this in mind.

BE GENEROUS: When you do give coaching, feedback, or constructive criticism, be kind and considerate. Think about whether your feedback is truly helpful. Keep your input focused on the storyteller and the question or story being discussed. Avoid using this as an opportunity to share your own similar story; there's a different time and place for that.

BE HONEST AND KIND: Give feedback the way you'd like to receive it. The idea of a "compliment sandwich" works well here: start with a compliment (what you appreciated), then offer your constructive criticism, and finish with another positive comment about their story, style, or delivery.

When we deny our
stories, they define us.
When we own our stories, we
get to write a brave
new ending."

—Brené Brown

"My Life in Paragraphs" Process

NOW FOR THE fun! You might want to grab a journal or notebook dedicated to jotting down your initial story notes. If you'd like, you can pick up the one I've made for you, which is available on Amazon: *My Life in Paragraphs Notebook: Exploring Your Stories.* You don't need to be a writer to tell good stories. My focus has always been on helping people tell spoken-word stories. If writing isn't your thing, bullet points work really well. Keep it simple and fun!

CHOOSE A PROMPT AND THEN CONSIDER:

VALUES: Reflect on your core values and list the top three to five that connect to this prompt. You can modify or update your list at any point during the process. [See page 170 for a list of values.]

BULLET NOTES: What personal stories does this prompt remind you of? Take time to jot down bullet points of the stories it brings to mind. Allow time to contemplate this part. Go for a walk, ponder over tea, discuss the prompt with friends. Allow yourself the space for your stories to surface.

YOUR STORY: Choose one story from your list to focus on, preferably the one that inspires you the most.

CHOICES: Make bullet-point notes of the choices you made related to this story.

VALUES: What values influenced your choices? Are they the same as what you originally selected? Update your list if needed.

TRANSFORMATION: How did this story change you? What did you learn?

GROWTH: How did this experience or situation affect your life or shape your future decisions?

PULLING IT ALL TOGETHER: Create a synopsis—or "Beat Sheet"—for your story. Practice your story a couple of times and then refine it by sharing it with someone you feel comfortable with. Notice their reactions and ask for constructive feedback. Take what helps you and leave the rest. It's your story, you have the final say in how it's told—instructions on how to create a "Beat Sheet" are on page 166.

YOUR STORY AS LEGACY: Take some time to think about who you would like to share your story with, both now and in the future. Write down their names.

GROUP GUIDELINES: You'll notice this process works best when you do it with others. Enjoy the new connection points you build with friends, family, coworkers, and maybe even strangers! When you turn to page 152, you'll see I have provided guidelines on how to create and run a storytelling duo or circle. Stories are more delicious when shared!

LET ME HELP: I facilitate in-person and virtual workshops using the "My Life in Paragraphs" process. Visit AprilBell.com to learn more.

Scan code
for workshop

"The truth is a story we

tell ourselves."

—Thomas King

Storytelling Tips

HERE'S THE THING about stories—at their core, each is simply a narrative with a beginning, a middle, and an end. That's it. It's the best place to start. Don't get too caught up in being perfect at the beginning. As you develop your own style, you might want to try some of the ideas I'm sharing here to make your stories more engaging. Like most things, the more you practice storytelling, the better you'll get.

KEEP IT REAL: People often ask me, "What's the secret sauce to telling a great story?" One of the biggies is being authentic and vulnerable. People connect with our stories on a much deeper level when we're honest about what happened and how we truly felt in the moment.

Now, vulnerability can sometimes feel a bit nerve-wracking. I'm not suggesting you share more than feels safe or comfortable, but I do encourage you to be a little braver than usual in speaking your truth. Often, what we think makes us look weak or foolish is exactly what others see as our hidden strength and courage. Try testing the waters as you go, leaning in just a bit further than you normally would. The more open and authentic you allow yourself to be, the more you might surprise yourself with the impact your stories have on others. There's something about telling stories with an open heart that naturally draws people in.

KEEP A GENERAL FOCUS: Try to avoid too many tangential details. If you're a talker like me, you might tend to go off on tangents when telling a story. While this can work well in casual conversation, it can kill your story's flow. Notice when you start sharing details that could be their own separate stories. Either drop that part or find a quick way to wrap up your tangent and stay on track with your main storyline.

SHOW THE CONFLICT OR STRUGGLE: Contrast is key in making a good story great. What's at stake for you? Why does what happens in your story truly matter? If you can't answer this, you might want to consider finding a different story. Visit TheMoth.org to explore inspiring examples of how to effectively show the conflict.

START IN THE ACTION: Hook your listener right from the start by dropping them directly into your experience. Again, The Moth offers great examples of this on their website and YouTube channel.

BE AN ETHICAL STORYTELLER: Don't tell other people's stories. Personal storytelling is exactly that; it's personal to you and your perspective and shows your learning experiences. If you need to share someone else's story to make your point, be sure to tell that part of the story the way the person would have wanted it told.

KEEP IT LIGHT: Try not to tell others what to do or how to live. If you want to share wisdom, let it come through naturally in the stories you tell about your own life. Science has shown that one powerful way humans learn is by listening to engaging stories.

PULLING IN THE PAST: Don't forget to include photos! If you have pictures of yourself, others, or the places from your story—especially from that time period—they add so much depth to the listener's experience.

If you choose to use my StoryCatcher® app to film yourself or a friend sharing a story, you can add those photos, right inside the app. You can even create a photo slideshow using just your audio, where your photos replace the video while your voice narrates the story—great if you prefer not to be on camera. Photos really help bring your stories to life! You can find StoryCatcher® Pro on The Apple App Store.

"The stories we tell about ourselves and our families help us to make sense of our experiences, and to find meaning and purpose in our lives."

—Marshall Duke

Sharing Your Stories

WHEN YOU BEGIN sharing your personal stories, remember that everyone has their own unique style and voice, which is what makes storytelling so engaging and fun. Focus on being honest and heartfelt when sharing your experiences. I can't say this often enough—don't be afraid to be vulnerable. Let your emotions show in your storytelling. This will truly connect you with your listeners, making your story memorable. Being vulnerable, along with being a good listener, is key to building deeper connections through stories.

Something important to keep in mind about vulnerability is that you need to be discerning about what you're willing to share and with whom. I don't show the same level of vulnerability with acquaintances as I do with my closest friends. That's why having a trusted story buddy or storytelling circle is so valuable. You can practice your stories and identify your edges—those points where you feel unsure or exposed. If you're sharing something you haven't fully worked out for yourself, I don't recommend sharing it widely. You'll know you're ready when you can share that vulnerable piece without it overly impacting you emotionally. When you find that sweet spot, you'll see that your vulnerability becomes your story's greatest strength, and it encourages others to open up to you, too.

Storytelling is a two-way street. The people you're sharing with are there to listen and connect with you on a human level. Just be yourself and speak from the heart. Share your experiences, emotions, fears, joys, and triumphs. Focus on simply being you, and everything else will fall into place. Often, a detail I've hesitated to share turns out to be the one that makes the biggest impact!

Remember, storytelling is a skill that takes time and practice to develop. Don't be too hard on yourself if your first try doesn't go exactly as you imagined. Keep practicing, and you'll get better with each story you tell. And who knows? You might even inspire someone else to share their own story in the process!

Creating a Beat Sheet

NOW THAT YOU'RE ready to organize and tell your story, here's some guidance on how to do it. You might choose to do this with just one person, in a small group, or even on the stage!

Using the bits you've gathered through the "My Life in Paragraphs" process, create a beat sheet to help remember the key moments of your story. A beat sheet is a tool storytellers use to map out the sequence of a story, scene by scene. While it's often associated with screenwriting, it can also help storytellers craft a clear, well-structured tale.

Below, I use Bernadette Jiwa's story structure as an effective method to build a well-organized and emotionally compelling personal story. By following these steps and creating a beat sheet, you can ensure that your story is engaging, impactful, and memorable.

- Describe the time and setting of your story.

- Introduce the main people involved in your story.

- Identify the event or decision that kicks off your story.

- Introduce the conflict or problem that you faced.

- Describe your struggle to resolve this conflict.

- Show how facing the conflict changed you.

- Share any insights or lessons you learned as a result of your experience.

- End your story with a message that connects with the listener.

Once you've crafted your beat sheet, use it as a guide to help you tell your story. Make sure each scene focuses on advancing the story and engaging the listener.

Again, it's your story, and you get to decide how it's told. Often, I choose to cut the last two bullet points from the list above. This makes space for the listener to draw their own insights based on what they experienced while hearing my story.

If you pick up the *My Life in Paragraphs Notebook: Exploring Your Stories* (available on Amazon), you can use it to develop your stories further. Then, use the "Story Notes" pages in this book (located to the left of each story prompt) to write in your Beat Sheet. Doing so will allow this book to serve as your "Story Library."

"Stories can conquer fear, you know. They can make the heart bigger."

—Ben Okri

Exploring Your Values

WHEN I WORK with people on their stories, values often come up naturally—which is my favorite part. There's something about values-based stories that reveals not just what happened, but what's truly important to someone and the wisdom behind their choices. These values typically fall into two categories that are helpful to understand.

Core values are the fundamental beliefs that guide how we make decisions and live our lives. These are usually shaped by our upbringing, our culture, and the experiences we've had. Things like honesty, integrity, respect, responsibility, fairness— the principles that feel non-negotiable to us. When you include your core values in your stories, you're essentially letting people know what you stand for.

Then there are what are called **intrinsic values**—the things we treasure simply for what they are, not for what they can do for us. Love, compassion, creativity, personal growth, the way beauty moves us. These are the qualities that bring meaning to our lives just by existing. When these show up in your stories, they tend to inspire people and help them think about what brings them joy and fulfillment.

When you weave both types of values into your storytelling, you're not just retelling what happened to you—you're sharing the principles and experiences that have shaped your life. You're building bridges that can reach across generations and perspectives, giving what matters most to you a chance to touch others and live on. Your stories become more than just memories; they become a meaningful legacy that can inspire anyone who hears them.

Values You May Hold

accountability	commitment	diversity
achievement	community	education
adaptability	compassion	empathy
adventure	competition	enthusiasm
altruism	confidence	equality
ambition	connection	ethics
authenticity	contentment	excellence
balance	contribution	entrepreneurship
beauty	cooperation	fairness
belonging	courage	faith
career	creativity	family
caring	curiosity	forgiveness
citizenship	dignity	freedom
collaboration	discipline	friendship

fun	kindness	security
future-generations	knowledge	self-discipline
generosity	leadership	self-expression
grace	learning	self-respect
gratitude	legacy	safety
growth	leisure	serenity
harmony	love	service
health	loyalty	simplicity
home	mindfulness	stewardship
honesty	modesty	success
humor	nature	spirituality
humility	order	time
hope	optimism	teamwork
inclusion	patience	tradition
idealism	parenting	transparency
integrity	peace	travel
intelligence	perseverance	truth
innovation	philanthropy	tolerance
innocence	pride	understanding
individuality	privacy	uniqueness
independence	respect	vision
initiative	reliability	vulnerability
intuition	resilience	well-being
joy	responsibility	wealth
justice	risk-taking	wisdom

"The stories we tell each other have the power to heal or to wound. They also have the power to connect us to one another in deep and meaningful ways."

—Mark Nepo

Stories are Gifts

EVERYONE HAS A unique story to tell, one worth sharing. Your experiences, struggles, triumphs, and lessons can serve as a source of inspiration, comfort, guidance, and hope for others facing similar challenges. Sharing your story can be a cathartic and empowering experience. It helps you reflect on your past, gain a better understanding of yourself, and possibly find closure. Equally important, telling your story can make a real difference in others' lives.

Personal storytelling is a powerful way to help preserve and understand our shared history. As a method of recording firsthand accounts and experiences, it provides unique insights into historical events from the perspectives of everyday people. It can capture cultural nuances and forgotten details that might otherwise be lost. It gives voice to marginalized communities and offers a more inclusive view of history. By sharing your personal stories, you can bridge generational gaps and cultural differences, cultivate empathy, leading to a deeper understanding of who you are and where you come from. Personal storytelling also enriches historical research, helping create a fuller, more accurate picture of our collective human experience.

On a smaller scale, your story might resonate with someone going through a tough time. Hearing how you overcame a challenge could offer hope and motivate them to keep going. It might help them feel less alone and more understood.

Telling your story can break down barriers and promote empathy and understanding across different backgrounds. By opening up, you give others a glimpse into your world, bridging divides. I believe that personal storytelling has the power to change the world. In my work as an interviewer, the more diverse my client circle becomes, the more I see we're more alike than different.

I find this true in professional settings too, where we tend to hide behind roles and titles. When a leader shares a story about a time they failed and what they learned, or when a team member talks about an experience that shaped their work ethic, something shifts— the workplace feels more human. These stories become gifts that build trust, foster understanding, and create the kind of open culture where everyone can do their best work.

Don't hesitate to share your stories. Your words could have a powerful impact on someone else's life, and sharing your stories could become one of the most rewarding things you ever do.

"Storytelling is how we make sense of the world. It is how we share our experiences and connect with others."

—Mark Nepo

"Through exploring our own sacred stories, we shape the foundations which hold up our future generations."

—April Bell

Life Stories Case Study

IN SPRING 2014, my spiritual daughter Carli Mason gathered two case studies to illustrate the value of life story work for a college course she was taking. Not only did she unearth the benefits for the storyteller, but also for the story catcher. The first interview is with Elizabeth, our reluctant storyteller from earlier. The second interview is with me and shows my perspective as the "catcher" of life stories.

I am deeply touched by the high praise Elizabeth gives me in the following interview, and I hope including it here doesn't come across as self-aggrandizing. I love what she shared with Carli about our time together, as it beautifully illustrates the value of exploring one's personal stories.

Carli [C] and Elizabeth [E]:

[C] How did you find out about April and her business, Tree of Life Legacies?

[E] My son, Peter, connected me to April when he contracted with her to do a video of my life. I am so very grateful for that introduction, because April is now my great friend—loving, compassionate, empathic, enthusiastic, and fun-loving.

[C] What compelled you to have a video biography made?

[E] Peter compelled me, and I was a bit reluctant at the time, as I felt there wasn't much of interest to tell, that I had led a pretty ordinary life. In the end, I was so happy that I agreed, because not only did others think I had something to say and had led a pretty interesting life, but I also felt that way—a great transformation for me!

[C] How has April's work helped you share your family stories?

[E] April is brilliant in her work! She knows how to ask questions, which questions to ask, and how to elicit answers. And she is a profound listener—masterful! Her work was the catalyst not only for my sharing the stories seen and heard on her video, but also the inspiration for me to continue to write my stories as well. I am now writing "My Life in Paragraphs" for my kids.

[C] Has the work done with April brought your family closer? If so, how?

[E] My family and I have always been very close, but April helped create a platform for a more enriched dialogue and a greater desire to continue sharing stories, and this brings us even closer.

[C] Why do you feel it is important to share stories with future generations?

[E] This is a magnificent way to forge a road and a deep connection between the past and the future. Though the technological world is wonderful in so many ways, it has, I believe, diminished the personal and very intimate ways in which we used to communicate. We now send emails, post on Facebook, etc., and rarely write letters or record our thoughts and lives in journals. We are often too busy or distracted to simply sit with each other and share our stories orally and intimately. I fear we could "lose" ourselves, and future generations would know little or nothing about the family that came before them, and even worse, CARE little about who and what preceded them. We could become the lost generations.

Carli [C] and April [A]:

[C] What persuaded you to get started in making video biographies?

[A] In late 2007/early 2008, I was at a crossroads in my life and really seeking what to do next professionally. I knew I wanted to do work with purpose, to work with passion. I had done a lot of research on the matter.

During that same time, my dad brought up an idea we

had discussed in the past. In 2000 my grandfather had passed away. He and my grandmother both were fantastic storytellers and hysterically funny in sharing the family stories in their tag-team fashion at dinner parties and family gatherings.

Feeling the loss of being able to experience that any longer with them together, my dad suggested that we do an audio recording of my grandmother sharing the stories and then marry her audio stories with old family photos, adding screen text and music throughout. Well, not long after, she had a stroke and was afflicted with the condition known as aphasia, which leaves the person cognitively aware, but when they speak, gibberish comes out. It was heartbreaking to witness such an amazing storyteller having to deal with this for the rest of her days. We never recorded her stories.

Back to 2008. My dad suggested I explore the idea of capturing stories for other families. Around the same time, I was working with a coach who helped people find their true professional calling in life. At the end of that coaching engagement, it was crystal clear that the perfect vocation for me was to create personal history films, doing video interviews with people so they could pass on their ancestry—their family stories and traditions—while also sharing their values and philosophies.

[C] Why do you feel that it is important to share stories with future generations?

[A] In March of 2013, I found an article in The New York Times titled "The Stories That Bind Us." When I read that article, all I said was, "EXACTLY!" I highly recommend reading it.

I feel we need to know where we came from in order to feel supported and guided in where we choose to go in our lives. Sharing stories with future generations provides us with a greater sense of connection to the people in our lives and those who came before us. It gives us comfort, guidance, inspiration, and hope. ASKING our elders to share those stories gives them a deeper sense of meaning to their own lives and a sense that they truly DO MATTER, that their lives have been of value, and that their learning and the legacy of who they are can and will live on even after their physical body is gone from this earth.

[C] Do you feel that your work creates a better sense of meaning of life for others? If so, how?

[A] I think it creates a deeper understanding of who we are as individuals. When we understand that, we are able to live and love more fully in good times and bad.

[C] How does hearing stories about others help us with our own personal lives?

[A] It provides love and connection. It gives us comfort, support, inspiration, guidance, and hope.

[C] Why is it important for the storyteller to express not only the ups but the downs in their life as well?

[A] This provides hope. It's my belief that in this life, without hope, we have nothing. It shows us the reality of life and reminds us that we are not alone when things get tough. When we see how someone we love or are related to has persevered through a great tragedy or difficulty, it empowers us to persevere through our own trials, hopefully with grace.

[C] What aspects of your job do you most enjoy, and which are the most challenging?

[A] I LOVE the interview. I am gifted with the privilege to connect with each storyteller completely, listen to them deeply, and witness them going on the amazing journey that is the unique life they have lived. And then the self-acknowledgment and awareness that transpire through that telling are nothing short of extraordinary. It's pure magic, each and every single time.

The challenging part is when people postpone getting the interview complete. We all seem to think we're immortal. Until we're not. I've had more than one person postpone getting the interview scheduled and then have the opportunity lost due to death or illness. In the case of folks who wanted to have their parent or grandparent share their story, there's a lot of regret there: "Why didn't I do it when I first thought of it?"

[C] If a potential client were to tell you that they do not have interesting stories to tell, what would be your response?

[A] I tell them about Elizabeth. So many people say that they don't have anything to say or share. Everyone has a story to tell. Everyone. And we (the kids and others) WANT TO KNOW! That person knows things about the people in their life and those who came before them that, if left undocumented, will be lost forever. Often, we don't realize how extraordinary we are; we do what we do because that's what comes naturally to us.

Once storytellers sit down and begin to witness themselves from a different perspective, they see how incredible their own resilience is, the depth of the love they've shared through their lives, the people they've impacted, and those who have had an impact on them. It's nothing short of a profound healing journey for the storytellers and the people in their lives (and those in the future) who get to hear their stories.

About the Author

EVER SINCE I can remember, I've loved listening to people's stories. When I was a child, my mom called me "the visitor" because I'd run off most days to visit whatever elder neighbor would have me.

That's me in the photo.

The homes on the small lane where I grew up in the San Francisco East Bay were mostly occupied by an older generation. I've always been interested in people, stories, and creativity.

In the early 1990s, I started my media career in the fast-paced, exciting, and deadline-intense world of major daily newspapering. I also earned my degree in psychology. My newspaper career lasted fourteen years, during which I held leadership roles on the production-graphics side, prepress.

In 2008, I had the opportunity to reinvent my path and stepped into my current passion as a values-based storytelling guide. As a young person, I never could have imagined how the core skills I developed in early adulthood would intersect; today, I blend my background in psychology, leadership experience, and the graphics and technical skills from my early career.

Being the daughter of an artist and a mobile tech pioneer, I am inspired to help others creatively tell their stories through technology. Since 2008, I have been gently guiding people to connect with their true essence and skillfully capture that on video.

Over the years, I've refined my listening skills, as I am a natural at deeply connecting with others. I help people craft the stories that matter to them most. My clients include families, professionals, individuals, and businesses that value the power of story.

What excites me these days is helping people discover the alchemical power of personal storytelling through workshops and retreats. My focus is mainly on spoken-word stories, so people daunted by writing love my process.

I am an innovator, recognized by The New York Times, USAToday, WIRED, and others for bringing ethical will and legacy storytelling to the masses through the co-creation of StoryCatcher® for iPhone, launched in 2013. For nearly twelve years and running, our app has helped thousands capture and share their most cherished stories on video.

For fun, I enjoy riding my mountain bike, trekking in the High Sierra, and exploring the mysteries of the human spirit and condition.

Ultimately, our stories are what connect and bind us, today and into the future. What's *your* story?

Resources and Bibliography

Resources

Do-It-Yourself:

Create memorable keepsake videos with your stories! Download StoryCatcher® Pro from The Apple App Store. You can film yourself (or a friend), add photos, screen text, plus a title card. You can even assemble a collection of stories to make a full documentary, right inside the app.

Visit StoryCatcher.app to learn more about this simple yet powerful tool for personal storytelling.

Let Me Help:

I lead in-person and virtual workshops using the "My Life in Paragraphs" process. I am available to facilitate on-site retreats worldwide. Visit AprilBell.com to learn more.

 Scan code to download
StoryCatcher®

Scan code to visit
AprilBell.com

Bibliography

Angelou, Maya. *I Know Why the Caged Bird Sings*. New York: Random House, 1969.

Brown, Brené. *Daring Greatly: How the Courage to Be Vulnerable Transforms the Way We Live, Love, Parent, and Lead*. New York: Gotham Books, 2012.

Brown, Brené. *The Gifts of Imperfection: Let Go of Who You Think You're Supposed to Be and Embrace Who You Are*. Center City, MN: Hazelden Publishing, 2010.

Jiwa, Bernadette. *What Great Storytellers Know: Seven Skills to Spark Your Creativity and Transform Your Life*. Vancouver: Page Two Books, 2020.

Nepo, Mark. *The Book of Awakening: Having the Life You Want by Being Present to the Life You Have*. San Francisco: Conari Press, 2000.

Nepo, Mark. *The One Life We're Given: Finding the Wisdom That Waits in Your Heart*. New York: Atria Books, 2016.

Oliver, Mary. *The Summer Day in New and Selected Poems*, 1992. Boston: Beacon Press, 1992.

Oliver, Mary. *Upstream: Selected Essays*. New York: Penguin Press, 2016.

Tsuchihashi, Rumi. *I Want to Remember This: Recognizing the Tiny Moments That Make Up a Life*. Seattle: Inside Out Living Books, 2021.

Zak, Paul. *Wired for Story: The Writer's Guide to Using Brain Science to Hook Readers from the Very First Sentence*. New York: Plume, 2012.

Acknowledgments

THANK YOU TO each and every person who has supported me on this journey. Many have gifted me with their wisdom and guidance, both named and unnamed. To those who ignited the spark: Sherri, Urs, Peter, Don, Thomas, Elizabeth, Carli, Sean, Dan, Arthur, Saul, Bojana, as well as my friends and colleagues from The Association of Personal Historians, especially Rob Cooper. Thanks to those who helped me create this book, which I never imagined in a million years I would write: Kendra, Ann, Pamela, Laurie, Nina, Marjorie, and more. The kind and powerful women in my Artist's Way Collective: Meridian, Desiree, Melaina, and Leah. The talented and generous folks at Story Republic: Bernadette, Anne, Rumi, Leanne, Michael, Michelle, Annie, Sabah, Terry, Carolyn, Andrea, Kellie, Gary, and others. Last but not least, Diana Rowan, for bringing alchemy to the party! I'm grateful and honored to have each of you as part of my story.